Easy Spanish Phrases Book

Over 1000 Phrases And Words For Everyday

CONTENT

INTRODUCTION

Let's get to know Spain first?Spain is one of the European countries bordered to the north by France, Andorra and the Bay of Biscay, to the south and east by the Mediterranean Sea, and to the northwest and west by the Atlantic Ocean and Portugal. It also includes the cities of Ceuta and Melilla in North Africa (specifically Morocco).

Why should you learn Spanish? As we know, the country of Spain is within the European Union. If you learn the Spanish language, it will make you special. Learning languages also helps to develop the human personality and helps to develop skills of creative thinking, imagination, innovation and thinking in general. It also helps to communicate, as we know that communication and the ability to communicate the idea, no matter how important it is. Very in our time, and acquiring this ability requires effort. Learning languages helps increase the ability to focus, analyze information, strengthen memory, and enhance human cognitive abilities, whether in children or adults.

That is why we advise you to learn languages, whatever your age. Therefore, we offer you this book. You will learn to write and speak fluently in Spanish, step by step. The curriculum we followed in creating this book will develop your level in the Spanish language, whether you are a be-

FOREWORD

this new book is aimed at students and anyone want to learn spanish. it is composed of several parts

▷ simple words to generally identify the language.

▷ how to pronounce words are used (numbers- colors - words used in daily life).
the vocabulary guide.

▷ simple dialogs are simple examples that help develop the person's understanding.

each part has

▷ a test to assess your level.

▷ When you pass all the tests, you will be able to write and speak
fluent Spanish.

At first we will try to learn the structure of sentences step by step, and from them we will learn the pronunciation of letters

Let's start by pronouncing the letters in the Spanish accent

A	⟶ AH		Q	⟶ KOO
B	⟶ BEH		R	⟶ EHRE
C	⟶ SHE		S	⟶ EHSE
D	⟶ DEH		T	⟶ TEN
E	⟶ EH		U	⟶ OOO
F	⟶ ENFEH		V	⟶ UNBEH
G	⟶ HEH		W	⟶ DOUBLE U
H	⟶ AHCHE		X	⟶ EHQUISE
I	⟶ EE		Y	⟶ EEGRIEGA
J	⟶ HOTA		Z	⟶ SEHTA
K	⟶ KAH			
L	⟶ ELEH			
M	⟶ ENME			
N	⟶ ENNE			
O	⟶ OH			
P	⟶ PEH			

Let's get acquainted with some words in the Spanish language through which we will learn the pronunciation of letters

A	amigo	friend
B	beso	kiss
C	casa	house
ch	chica	girl

prounounce chice like tchika

D	dedo	finger
E	escoba	broom
F	flor	flower
G	guante	glove
H	helado ice c	ream
I	isla	island
J	jugo	juice

pronounce jugo like khogo j will be kh

K	kiwi	kiwi
L	libro	book
M	mesa	table
N	naris	nose
O	ola	wave

P	pan	bread
Q	queso	chess
R	ropa	clothers
S	silla	chess
T	taza	cup
U	uva	grape
V	Ventana	window
W	windsurf	windsurf
X	xilofono	xylophone

pronounce silophono

Y	yoyo	yo-yo
Z	zabato	shoe

In the English language, we extend the letters
during their pronunciation. In the Spanish language,
we press on the letters during their pronunciation.

Try to repeat the pronunciation of the words over
and over until you learn the tone of the Spanish letters

simple sentence installation

In this part we will try to learn how to link words
together and form useful sentences

It's Normal = es normal
It's abnormal = no es normal   no negation tool
Importante = es importante
Para mi = for me   para = for   mi = me
Es para mi
No es para mi
Let's try to connect importante with para mi :
Es importante para mi = it's important for me
Hoy = oy in sapanish   h It is not pronounced
if the first word comes
Es imporante hoy = it's importante to day
No Es imporante hoy = it's not importante to day

Each time we will mention new words and link them
together to get useful sentences used in daily life in
order to enrich the knowledge balance

Samething = algo
Samething important = algo importante
It's samething important = es algo importante
es algo importante para mi = It's samething
important for me
es imposible = it's imposible
no es imposible = it's not imposible
algo imposible = samething imposible

ahora = in this moment
hora in Spanish meaning watch
ahora es imposible = it's imposible now
es imposible hoy = it's imposible to day
nada = nothing
nada es imposible para mi = nothing imposible
for me
hoy es importante para mi = today is important
for me
perfect = perfecto
es perfecto = it's perfect
asi = like that
ahora es perfecto asi = now is perfect like this

8

ahora es perfecto asi = now is perfect like this
ahora no es importante = now is not important
"no" The negation is always before the verb
If you pronounce this sentence, you will feel that
it is one word, as if there are no spaces
Muy = very
Es muy importante = it's very important
Es muy importante para mi = it's very important
for me
Hoy es muy importante para mi = to day it's very
important for me
Bueno = good
Es bueno = it's good
No es bueno = it's not good
Es muy bueno = it's very good
No es muy bueno = it's not good
The slash above any character indicates that that
character must be pressed
Fantàstico = fantastic
Asi
Es fantàstico para mi = it's fantastic for me
Es fantàstico asi = it's fantastic like that
9

Aqui = here

Es fantàastico aqui = it's fantastic here

Es algo fantàstico = it's samething fantastic

To ask the question you must change the tone
of voice

¿Es para mi? = it's for me

¿Es normal? = it's normal ?

¿Es algo importante?

A question begins with an inverted question mark
and ends with a regular question mark

Estar aqui = is here

Es importante estar aqui hoy = it's important to be
her to day

Es fantàstico estar aqui hoy = it's fantastic to be her
to day

Es muy boeno estar aqui hoy = it's very good to be
her to day

Hacer = act   meaning "do" You will understand the
meaning of the word more in the examples

Verb with a pronoun   "hacerlo"

Es importante hacerlo = it's important to do that.

Es imposible hacerlo = it's imposible to do that
Necesito = need
No nesicito = I don't need
 necisito hacerlo = need to do that
no necisito hacerlo = no need to do that

necisito esta aqui ahora = need to be here now
porque = why , because
¿porque es importante = why is important?
 Porque es importnate = because important
Necesito hacerlo hoy porque es importante
=
Need to make It in today because is important
Necesito estar aqui hoy porque es importante
=
need to be here to day because is important
Saber = know
Necesito saber = need to know
Si = if
Si = yes
Si esposible para mi = if possible for me...
Necesito saber si es possible = need to know
if possible

Necesito saber si es posible hacerlo ahora porque
es muy importante = need to know if possible to
make it now because is very important
Necesito saber si es algo importante = need to know
if samething important
Quiero = want
Quiero hacerlo = want to do that
Quiero hacerlo hoy = want to do that today
Quiero hacerlo ahora = want to do that now
No quiero = does not want
Quiero saber si es possible = want to know if
possible
Y = and
Es importante y ncesito saber = it's important
and I need to know
Es importante para mi y necesito saber si es posible
hacerlo hoy = it's important for me and I need to
know if possible make it in today
Es importante para mi y quiero saber si es posible
hacerlo hoy = it's important for me and I want to
know if possible make it in today

Salir = out

Necesito asir ahora = need to get out

Qiero salir hoy = want to get out today

Esta = this

Noche = night

Quiero salir esta noche = want to get out this night

No Quiero salir esta noche = I don't want to get out this night

Tengo que = must to...

Tengo que salir = I have (must) to get out

Tengo que salir esta noch = I have (must) to get out this night

Tengo que estar aqui = I have to be here

Tengo que estar aqui esta noche = I have to be here this night

Numbers :

0	cero	seh roh
1	uno	oo noh
2	dos	dohss
3	tres	trehss
4	cuatro	kwah roh
5	cinco	seen koh
6	seis	sayss
7	siete	see eh teh
8	ocho	oh choh
9	nueve	nweh veh
10	diez	dee ess
11	once	ohn seh
12	doce	doh seh
13	trece	treh seh
14	catorce	kah tor seh
15	quince	keen seh
16	dieciséis	dee eh see sayss
17	diecisiete	dee eh see see eh teh
18	dieciocho	dee eh see oh choh

19	diecinueve	dee eh see nweh veh
20	veinte	vayn teh
21	veintiuno	vayn tee oo noh
22	veintidós	vayn tee dohss
30	treinta	trayn tah
31	treinta y uno	trayn tah ee oo noh
32	treinta y dos	trayn tah ee dohss
40	cuarenta	kwah ren tah
50	cincuenta	seen kweh tah
60	sesenta	seh sen tah
70	setenta	seh ten tah
80	ochenta	oh chen tah
90	noventa	noh ven tah
100	cien	see en
101	ciento uno	see en toh oo noh
102	ciento dos	see en toh dohss
200	doscientos	dohss see en tohss
300	trescientos	trehss see en tohss
400	cuatrocientos	kwah troh see en tohss
500	quinientos	kee nee en tohss
600	seiscientos	sayss see en tohss

700	setecientos	eh teh see en tohss
800	ochocientos	oh choh see en tohss
900	novecientos	noh veh see en tohss
1000	mil	meel
2000	dos mil	dohss meel
100000	cien mil	see en meel
1000000	millon	mee yohn
2000000	dos millones	dohs mee yoh ness

Colors :

The color = el color
Red = rojo
Orange = naranja
Yellow = Amarillo
Green = verde
Blue = azul
Purple = lila
Pink = rosa
Brown = marron
Black = negro
White = blanco
Light = claro
Dark = oscuro

16

A:¿Qué color te gusta usar en tu ropa?=
What color do you like to use in your clothes.
B:De hecho, el color negro es genial. Pero no con
toda la ropa me gustan los zapatos negros=In fact,
the black color is great. But not in all clothes I like
black shoes.
A:En cuanto al resto de la ropa, la mayoría son de
colores oscuros=As for the rest of the clothes,
most of them are dark colors.
B:Esto es genial, también me gustas=This is great, I
like you too.
A:me encanta dibujar=love to draw.
B:Sí, dibujo en mi tiempo libre. Bueno, sé tu
pregunta, los colores que uso ahora son solo blanco
y negro=Yes, I draw in my spare time. Well, I know
your question, the colors I use now are only black
and white.
A:A diferencia de ti, trato de usar todos los colores,
esto le da al dibujo un aspecto impresionante=
Unlike you, I try to use all colors, this gives the
drawing an impressive look.

B:Correcto, solo tienes que dominar el uso de lápices de colores=Right, you just have to master the use of coloring pens.

A:Hago ejercicio todos los dias=I exercise daily

B:¿Qué piensas del concurso?=What do you think of the contest.

A:Esto es interesante, dime=This is interesting, tell me.

B:Cada uno de nosotros dibuja a su mejor amigo= Each one of us draw his best friend.

A:Sé que eres mi mejor amigo=I know you are my best friend.

B:Tú también eres mi mejor amigo=You are also my best friend.

A:Bueno, que comience el concurso=Well, let the contest begin.

Daily life :

daily life = vida diaria (morning) = (Mañana)

A:buenos dias=good morning

B:¿Hay desayuno?=Is there breakfast

A:Por supuesto, hijo mío, ven a la mesa.=Of course, my son, come to the table

B:Mañanas es hora de trabajar voy a trabajar mamá =Morning it's time to work I'm going to work mom

Abuena suerte mi hijo=Good luck my son

(afternoon) =(tarde)

B:buenas tardes mama=good afternoun mom

A:has vuelto hijo mio, como te fue en el trabajo hoy=you are back my son, How was work today

B:Como siempre mamá=As usual, mom

A:creo que tendras hambre=I think you will be hungry

B:si, mama mucha hambre=yes, mom very hungry

A:¿Qué harás después de comer?=What will you do after you eat?

B:voy a encontrarme con mi amigo=I'm going to meet my friend

A:por qué, está todo bien=why, is evrything ok

B:Sí, dijo que me necesita para un trabajo.=Yes, he said he needs me for some work

A:bien, no llegues tarde=ok, do not be late

(noche) = (night)

B:hola mamá=hy mom

A:hola, has vuelto a tiempo=hy, You are back on time

B:cené con mi amigo=I had dinner with my friend

A:Come un poco de la comida de tu mamá=Eat some of your mom's food

B:ok mamá lo haré=Ok mom I will

A:buenas noches hijo=good night son

B:buenas noches mamá=good night mom

Food :

food = comida
vegetables = vegetales
Potato = Papa
peas = guisantes
the bean = el frijol
the carrot = la zanahoria
the tomato = el tomate
fennel = hinojo
the artichoke = la alcachofa
the radish = el rábano
the pumpkin = la calabaza
squash = calabaza
the courgette = el calabacín
cauliflower = coliflor
the bean = el frijol
turnip = nabo
the leek = el puerro
endive = endibia
eggplant = berenjena
parsley = perejil
the lettuce = la lechuga

Fruta=fruit
Apple=manzana
the banana=el plátano
apricot=albaricoque
the strawberry=la fresa
the cherry=la cereza
the mango=el mango
pineapple=piña
The kiwi=El kiwi
the ship=el barco
The mandarin=el mandarín
the melon=el melon
the watermelon=la sandia
lychee=lychee
the lawyer=El abogado
the FIG=la figura
prickly pear=higo chumbo
the grape=la uva
the plum=la ciruela
the lemon=el limón
papaya=papaya
the radish=el rábano

the pear=la pera

estoy hambriento=i'm very hungry

Cuál es tu comida favorita=what is your favorite
food

me gusta comer fruta en la mañana=i like eat fruit
in morning

me gusta ir a la escuela sin comer brakfest=i like
going to school without eating brakfest

el desayuno es muy importante=breakfast is very
important

El almuerzo también es muy importante, ayuda
a completar el día=Lunch is very important too,
helpe to complete the day

Comer un poco de fruta en la cena mantiene el
cuerpo sano=Eating a little fruit at dinner keeps the
body healthy

comida fantástica en español:

Gazpacho

Tortilla Española

Croquetas

Patatas bravas

Gambas al ajillo

Paella
Fabada
Pulpo a la gallega
Pisto

Direction :

north=norte

east=este

West=oeste

South=Sur

Where are you heading today?=¿Hacia dónde te diriges hoy?

Where is the sports field?=¿Dónde está el campo de deportes?

Where is Spain?=¿Dónde está España?

Spain is located in the north of the country of Morocco (Morocco is located in the north of the continent of Africa)=España se encuentra en el norte del país de Marruecos (Marruecos se encuentra en el norte del continente africano)

Town centre=Centro de la ciudad

above=sobre

under=bajo

where do you live=Dónde vives

Above the medical clinic north of the city=Sobre
la clínica médica al norte de la ciudad.

I have a landfill under my house where I collect car
equipment=Tengo un vertedero debajo de mi casa
donde recojo equipos de automóviles.

right=derecho

left=izquierda

I use my right hand while writing=Uso mi mano
derecha mientras escribo

I use my left hand while writing=Uso mi mano
izquierda mientras escribo

Meeting :

how are you=¿cómo estás?

i'm fine and you=estoy bien, y tú

me too=Yo también

what are you doing=Que estas haciendo

work in same file =trabajar en el mismo archivo

let me help you=Deja que te ayude
oh thank you=Oh gracias
no problem=No hay problema

What is the family news?=¿Cuál es la noticia
de la familia?
Everything is okay=Todo está bien
I would like to invite you to dinner tomorrow=
Me gustaría invitarte a cenar mañana.
This is great, is there any occasion?=Esto es genial,
¿hay alguna ocasión?
Yes my wife is pregnant=si mi esposa esta
embarazada
I'm so happy for you, we'll definitely come=Estoy
tan feliz por ti, definitivamente vendremos.
we are waiting for you=te estamos esperando

Sport :

26

football=fútbol
Basketball=Baloncesto
Tennis Sport=tenis deporte
volleyball=vóleibol
handball=balonmano
Football=Fútbol americano
swimming=nadando
longitudinal jump=salto longitudinal
the speed race=la carrera de velocidad
the javelin=la jabalina
the weight drop=la caída de peso
judo=judo
fencing=Esgrima
volleyball=vóleibol
the bike race=la carrera de bicicletas
the hunt=la caza
Ping pong=ping pong
the horse race=la carrera de caballos
the box=la caja
baseball=béisbol
ski=esquí

surf=navegar

paragliding=parapente

Golf=Golf

What is your favorite sport=Cuál es su deporte
favorito

I like to play football=me gusta jugar al fútbol

I love watching tennis=me encanta ver tenis

Sports are very beneficial for health=El deporte es
muy beneficioso para la salud

Eating healthy meals and exercising is essential for
a healthy body=Comer alimentos saludables
y hacer ejercicio es esencial para un cuerpo sano

Culture :

Tell me about your culture=Háblame de tu cultura

i love spanish culture=amo la cultura española

Spain is famous all over the world=España es
famosa en todo el mundo

She is also famous for dancing=Ella también es
famosa por bailar

Do not forget the architectural buildings of Spain=No te olvides de los edificios arquitectónicos de España

Spain also has?=¿España también tiene?

artistic heritage.=patrimonio artístico.

Spanish architecture=patrimonio artístico.

classical guitar=guitarra clásica

Services :

I need to go to the coffee shop=tengo que ir a la cafeteria

hotel=hotel

hospital=hospital

Cinema=Cine

Resturant=restaurante

garden=jardín

the Secretary=le secrétaire

director=réalisateur

hairdresser=coiffeur

train=former

the bus=Le bus

the post office=la poste

Where is the cinema located?=¿Dónde está el cine?

The cinema is located in the city center=El cine está ubicado en el centro de la ciudad.

Thank you for your help=Gracias por tu ayuda

I want to ask you? Do you provide services in...=¿Quiero preguntarte? ¿Prestas servicios en...

Travel :

field=campo

the trees=los árboles

The peasant=el campesino

the cottage=la casa de Campo

the flock of sheep=el rebaño de ovejas

the farm=la granja

the sahara=El Sahara

The plain=El avion

the mountain=la montaña

the sky=el cielo

the sea=el mar

River=río
the snow=la nieve
the rain=la lluvia
spring=primavera
summer=verano
autumn=otoño
Winter=Invierno
the sun=el sol
the moon=la luna
Lake=lago
the waterfall=La cascada
camping=cámping
Where do you like to travel?=¿Dónde te gusta viajar?
I always like to get out of the city and go to the mountainous
areas=Siempre me gusta salir de la ciudad e ir a las zonas
montañosas
I love camping=me encanta acampar
Cool, I also hang out with my friends=Genial, también salgo
con mis amigos
Where are you camping?=¿Dónde estás acampando?
We often camp in the desert areas=A menudo acampamos
en las zonas desérticas

Family :

My Father=Mi padre

My mom=Mi mamá

My brother=Mi hermano

My sister=Mi hermana

My uncle=Mi tío

Aunty=Tía

my maternal uncle=mi tio materno

My aunt=Mi tia

serious=grave

my grandmother=mi abuela

my cousin=mi primo

my cousin=mi primo

Cousin=Prima

My cousin=Mi primo

I have one uncle and one aunt=tengo un tio y una tia

I love my grandfather and grandmother very much=quiero mucho a mi abuelo y a mi abuela

My cousin is five years old=mi prima tiene cinco años

My aunt is very nice to me=mi tía es muy amable conmigo

Weather :

Rainy weather=Clima lluvioso

the weather is sunny=el clima es soleado

the weather is cloudy=El clima esta nublado

The sky is beautiful today=El cielo está hermoso hoy.

I think it will rain=creo que lloverá

I like to play soccer in cloudy weather=me gusta jugar futbol cuando esta nublado

The sky is clear let's go for a walk=El cielo está despejado vamos a dar un paseo

The temperature is moderate today=La temperatura es moderada hoy

It's very cold=la temperatura es alta

The temperature is high=la temperatura es alta

In the winter the weather is cold, in the summer it is hot, but in the spring and autumn the weather is mild=En invierno el clima es frío, en verano hace calor, pero en primavera y otoño el clima es templado

Wait for the summer to go to the beach and play in the sand= Esperar al verano para ir a la playa y jugar en la arena

Compagne :

the trees=los árboles
plow the land=arar la tierra
The peasant=el campesino
the shepherd=el pastor
the cottage=la casa de Campo
the flock of sheep=el rebaño de ovejas
the cows=las vacas
hens=gallinas
the barnyard=el corral
the hoe=la azada
the farm=la granja
The tractor=el tractor
wheat=trigo
the dig=la excavación
River=río
well=bien
carriage=carro
the cart=el carro

saddle=sillín

the smile=la sonrisa

straw=Paja

the grains=los granos

the stable=el establo

the fork=El tenedor

the Beehive=la colmena

the dog=el perro

the dromedary=el dromedario

horse=caballo

I really like going to the village with my grandmother=me gusta mucho ir al pueblo con mi abuela

We have a farm with chickens and horses=Tenemos una granja con gallinas y caballos

We plant every year, that's fun=Plantamos todos los años, eso es divertido

Every year I wait for harvest time in order to work with my family on the farm=Todos los años espero el tiempo de la cosecha para poder trabajar con mi familia en la finca

Medical :

medical=médico
doctor=médico
the nurse=la enfermera
the hospital=el hospital
medication=medicamento
the syringe=la jeringa
the blouse=la blusa
the stethoscope=el estetoscopio
the operating room=el quirófano
the pharmacy=la farmacia
doctor's office=oficina del doctor
the medical prescription=la prescripcion medica
the patient=el paciente
the scanner=el escáner
ultrasound=ultrasonido
the ambulance=La ambulancia
I will go to the doctor=iré al médico
I feel a headache=siento dolor de cabeza
Where is the hospital located?=¿Dónde está ubicado el hospital?
Where can I get medicine?=¿Dónde puedo obtener
medicamentos?

We have suffered from the spread of viruses=Hemos sufrido la propagación de virus
Medical precautions must always be taken to protect ourselves and those around us=Siempre se deben tomar precauciones médicas para protegernos a nosotros mismos y a quienes nos rodean

the post office :

the post office=el correo
the post office=el correo
the mailbox=el buzon
the postage stamp=el sello postal
the postcard=la postal
the envelope=la envoltura
the letter=la carta
the computer=el ordenador
the postman=el cartero
the tompon=el tompón
the crate=la caja
the post office=el correo
the parcel=la parcela

37

the fax=el fax
the phone=el teléfono
the telephone office=la oficina de telefono
I want to send some messages to my dad=Quiero enviar algunos mensajes a mi papá
Can you lend me your computer?=¿Puedes prestarme tu computadora?

School :

school=colegio
the schoolbag=la mochila de la escuela
the backpack=la mochila
the pencil case=el estuche de lápices
pencil sharpener=sacapuntas
the pencil=el lápiz
the mechanical pencil=el lápiz mecánico
gum=goma
the eraser=la goma de borrar
the ink cartridge=el cartucho de tinta
ball-point pen=bolígrafo
the graduated ruler=la regla graduada
the tube of glue=el tubo de pegamento
the pair of scissors=el par de tijeras
the square=la plaza
the adhesive tape=la cinta adhesiva
notebook=computadora portátil
the book=el libro
the notebook=el cuaderno
the sponge=la esponja
the chalk stick=el palo de tiza
water paint=Pintura de agua

the palette=la paleta
gouache tubes=tubos de gouache
the coulor pencils=los lapices de colores
markers=marcadores
the brush=el pincel
leaf=hoja
the microscope=el microscopio
the globe=el mundo
earthly=terrenal
table=mesa
the rapporteur=el ponente
The compass=La brújula
Table=Mesa
the sticks=la campaña
calculator=calculadora
apron=delantal
ink=tinta
the slate=la pizarra
the cutter=el cortador
the library=la biblioteca
the teacher=el maestro
office=oficina

playground=patio de juegos

school=colegio

the class=la clase

I like to go to school=me gusta ir a la escuela

School is necessary for mental development=La escuela es necesaria para el desarrollo mental

It also helps us to find great friends=También nos ayuda a encontrar grandes amigos

I study in primary school=yo estudio en primaria

My dad bought me new school supplies=Mi papá me compró útiles escolares nuevos

Can you lend me your red pen?=¿Me prestas tu bolígrafo rojo?

i like your pencil case=me gusta tu estuche

Games :

Games=Juegos

the marbles=las canicas

spinning top=peonza

the hoop=el aro

hopscotch=rayuela

hide and seek=al escondite
the domino=el dominó
billiards or snooker=billar o snooker
pinball=pinball
failures=pinball
lego=Lego
blind man=ciego
the leapfrog=el salto
the yo yo=el yo-yo
video games=videojuegos
the kite=la cometa
the swing=el columpio
the keels=las quillas
frisbee=disco volador
the pedal boat=el bote de pedales
bumper cars=coches de choque
the circus=el circo
skipping card=saltando tarjeta
the scooter=el patinete
the skateboard=El patinador
ski=esquí

table football=futbolín
the puzzle=el rompecabezas
artistic skiing=esquí artístico
monopoly=monopolio
the carousel=el carrusel
What is your favorite game=Cual es tu juego favorito
I love to play Dominoes=me encanta jugar al domino
I always play a game with my friends hide and seek=Siempre
juego un juego con mis amigos al escondite
I want to play with you=quiero jugar contigo
Well do you know the rules of the game?=Bueno, ¿conoces las
reglas del juego?
Yes, I'll close my eyes and count to ten, and you have to hide=
Sí, cerraré los ojos y contaré hasta diez, y tienes que esconderte
let's play= vamos a jugar

Clothes :

clothes	:	ropa		
T-shirt	:	Camiseta de manga corta		
the dress	:	el vestido		
the pyjama	:	el pijama		
trousers	:	pantalones		
the skirt	:	la falda		
Jacket	:	Chaqueta		
the coat	:	el abrigo	Handbag	: Bolso
the tailor	:	el sastre	the backpacks	: las mochilas
ballerinas	:	bailarinas	the tie	: la corbata
Sneakers	:	Zapatillas		
the sandal	:	la sandalia		
the shoes	:	los zapatos		
the boot	:	la bota		
the sneakers	:	las zapatillas		
the scarf	:	la bufanda		
the cap	:	la tapa		
the beret	:	la boina		
gloves	:	guantes		

the socks	:	los calcetines
the sock	:	el calcetín
tights	:	medias
knitting	:	tejido de punto
underpants	:	calzoncillos
the underpants	:	los calzoncillos
the bra	:	el sujetador
the sweater	:	el suéter
the short	:	El corto
the parka	:	la parka
shirt	:	camisa
the down jacket	:	la chaqueta de plumas
the windbreaker	:	la cazadora
the butterfly knot	:	el nudo de la mariposa
the overalls	:	los monos
the uniform	:	el uniforme
the boots	:	las botas
the belt	:	el cinturón	blue jeans	: vaqueros azules
cap	:	gorra	vest	: chaleco
the shawl	:	el chal
sportswear	:	ropa de deporte
the veil		el velo

Jobs :

trades	:	vientos alisios
the sacred	:	lo sagrado
the repairman	:	el reparador
the fisherman	:	el pescador
the potter	:	el alfarero
cartoonist	:	dibujante
the flourist	:	el florista
the Baker	:	el panadero
the carpet seller	:	el vendedor de alfombras
the servant	:	el sirviente
the worker	:	el trabajador
the banker	:	el banquero
the lawyer	:	El abogado
the director	:	el director
the farmer	:	el granjero
The peasant	:	el campesino
the gardener	:	El jardinero
filmmaker	:	cineasta
the cameraman	:	el camarógrafo
journal it	:	diario

merchant	:	comerciante
the rescuer	:	el salvador
the tailor	:	el sastre
the photograph	:	la fotografía
the painter	:	el pintor
the potter	:	el alfarero
the firefighter	:	el bombero
the postman	:	el cartero
Carpenter	:	Carpintero
the welder	:	el soldador
the shiner	:	el ojo morado
the engineer	:	el ingeniero
doctor	:	médico
the dentist	:	el dentista
The veterinarian	:	el veterinario
pharmacy	:	farmacia
the nurse	:	la enfermera
the fishmonger	:	el pescadero
the butcher	:	el carnicero
the hairdresser	:	el estilista
the teacher	:	el maestro
the mistress	:	la amante

The tourist guide	:	la guía turística
the air hostess	:	la azafata
the pilot	:	El piloto
the pastry chef	:	el pastelero
the bus driver	:	El conductor del bus
the singer	:	el cantante
postman	:	cartero
the coffee boy	:	el chico del café
the truck driver	:	el camionero
the clown	:	el payaso
the policeman	:	el policía
the musician	:	El músico
the coach	:	el entrenador
the masseuse	:	el masajista
the dresser	:	el vestidor
the cooker	:	el cocinero
seller	:	vendedor

TEST N°1

Try to focus and remember the previous lessons
before answering any question

questions:

1-Try to pronounce the following letters

A	B	C	D	E
F	G	H	I	J
K	L	M	N	O
P	Q	R	S	T
U	V	W	X	Y
		Z		

Give each letter a word

A................................ B................................ C................................

D................................ E................................ F................................

G................................ H................................ I................................

J................................ K................................ L................................

M................................ N................................ O................................

P................................ Q................................ R................................

S................................ T................................ U................................

V................................ W................................ X................................

Y................................ Z................................

2-If the word is in English, translate it into Spanish, if it is in
   Spanish, translate it into English

It's Normal :..............................
It's abnormal :...........................
Importante :.............................
Para mi :.................................
Samething :..............................
ahora :..................................
nada :...................................
hoy :....................................
perfect :................................
asi :....................................
Muy :....................................
Bueno :..................................
Aqui :...................................
Hacer :..................................
need :...................................
saber :..................................
porque :.................................
Quiero :.................................

Esta :..........................
Noche :........................
Tengo que :...................
Mas tarde :....................
Puedo :........................
Y :............................
Salir :........................

51

3-Translate these sentences into Spanish

it's important for me

....

it's importante to day

....

it's not importante to day

....

Samething important

....

It's samething important

....

It's samething important for me

....

it's imposible

....

it's not imposible

....

samething imposible

....

it's imposible now

....

it's imposible to day

....

nothing imposible for me

....

today is important for me

....

now is perfect like this

....

now is not important

....

it's very important

....

it's very important for me

....

to day it's very important for me

....

it's very good

....

it's not good

....

it's fantastic for me...

it's fantastic like that

....

it's samething fantastic

....

it's important to be her to day

....

I don't need...

need to be here to day because is important

....

need to know if possible to make it now because is very important

....

....

need to know if samething important

....

want to do that today

....

want to get out today

....

I have (must) to get out this night

....

I have to be here this night

....

4-Try to form a meaningful sentence from the following words

Es mi importante para

....

No imporante Es hoy

....

importante algo

....

algo mi es para importante

....

imposible algo ....
imposible ahora es..
para mi nada imposible es

....

es mi importante para hoy

....

asi es perfecto ahora

....

importante no es ahora

....

importante muy Es

....

muy para importante mi Es

....

muy es para importante mi Hoy

....

muy Es bueno ....
fantàstico para Es mi

....

Es aqui estar hoy importante

....

estar Es hoy aqui fantàstico

....

muy Es estar hoy aqui boeno

....

Es hacerlo importante

....

hacerlo necisito

....

necisito no hacerlo

....

esta aqui necisito ahora

....

es Porque importnate

....

hoy porque Necesito importante hacerlo es

....

estar Necesito aqui es importante hoy porque

....

saber si possible es   Necesito

....

Necesito importante es posible ahora hacerlo porque es
saber si muy

....

....

saber Necesito es algo importante si

....

hacer Quiero lo...
es saber si possible Quiero

....

Es y saber importante necisito

....

posible Es mi y hoy necesito saber si es importante hacerlo para

....

....

asir ahora Necesito

....

4-The color
Red ....
Orange ....
Yellow ....
Green ....
Blue ....
Purple ....
Pink ....
Brown ....
Black ....
White ....
Light ....
Dark ....

5-write this following numbers

1 :.......................................

2 :.......................................

3 :.......................................

4 :.......................................

5 :.......................................

6 :.......................................

7 :.......................................

8 :.......................................

9 :.......................................

10 :.......................................

11 :.......................................

12 :.......................................

13 :.......................................

14 :.......................................

15 :.......................................

16 :.......................................

17 :.......................................

18 :.......................................

19 :.......................................

20 :.......................................

21 :.......................................

22 :.......................................

23 :.......................................

24 :.......................................

25 :.......................................

26 :.......................................

27 :.......................................

28 :.......................................

29 :.......................................

30 :.......................................

40 :.......................................

50 :.......................................

60 :.......................................

70 :.......................................

80 :.......................................

90 :.......................................

100 :.......................................

1000 :.......................................

100000 :.......................................

1000000 :.......................................

6-translate to spanish
good morning...
Is there breakfast

....

Good luck my son

....

good afternoun mom

....

As usual, mom...
I think you will be hungry

....

yes, mom very hungry

....

What will you do after you eat?

....

I'm going to meet my friend

....

ok, do not be late

....

hy, You are back on time

....

I had dinner with my friend

....

good night son

....

good night mom

....

food
Apple

....

the banana

....

apricot

....

the strawberry

....

the cherry

....

the mango

....

pineapple

....

The kiwi

....

the ship

....

The mandarin

....

the plum

....

the lemon

....

papaya

....

the radish

....

the pear

....

the melon

....

the watermelon

....

lychee

....

the lawyer

....

the FIG

....

prickly pear

....

the grape

....

deriction   West

....

north   South

....

east   above

....

under

right

left

meeting
how are you

i'm fine and you

me too

what are you doing

work in same file

let me help you

oh thank you

no problem

....

sport
football

....

Basketball

....

Tennis Sport

....

volleyball

....

handball

....

Football

....

swimming

....

longitudinal jump

....

the speed race

....

the javelin

....

the weight drop

....

judo

....

fencing

....

volleyball

....

the bike race

....

the hunt

....

Ping pong

....

the horse race

....

the box

....

baseball

....

ski

....

surf

....

paragliding

....

Golf

....

culture
Tell me about your culture

....

i love spanish culture

....

Spain is famous all over the world

....

She is also famous for dancing

....

Do not forget the architectural buildings of Spain

....

Spain also has?

....

artistic heritage

....

Spanish architecture

....

classical guitar

....

Services
hotel :..
hospital :...
Cinema :..
Resturant :...
garden :...
the Secretary :...
director :...
hairdresser :...
train :..
the bus :..
66

the post office...

travel :...

field :...

the trees :...

The peasant :...

the cottage :...

the flock of sheep :..

the farm :..

the sahara :..

The plain :...

the mountain :..

the sky :..

the sea :..

River :..

the snow :..

the rain :...

spring :...

summer :..

autumn :..

Winter :..

the sun :..

the moon :.. 67

Lake :..

the waterfall :...

camping :..

family

My Father :..

My mom :...

My brother :..

My sister :...

My uncle :..

Aunty :...

my maternal uncle :...

My aunt :..

serious :...

my grandmother :...

my cousin :..

my cousin :..

Cousin :...

My cousin :..

Colors

Red   : ....

Orange   : ....

Yellow   :...................................

Green   :...................................

Blue   :...................................

Purple   :...................................

Pink   :...................................

Brown   :...................................

Black   :...................................

White   :...................................

Light   :...................................

Dark   :...................................

weather

the rain   :...........................

snow   :...........................

the clouds :...........................

the sun   :...........................

spring   :...........................

Winter   :...........................

the sky   :...........................69

compagne

the trees :..

plow the land :..

The peasant :...

the shepherd :...

the cottage :..

the flock of sheep :...

the cows :...

hens :...

the barnyard :..

the hoe :...

the farm :..

The tractor :..

wheat :...

the dig :..

River :..

well :..

carriage :..

the cart :...

saddle :..

the smile :...

straw :..70

the grains :...

the stable :..

the fork :..

the Beehive :...

the dog :...

the dromedary :...

horse :..

medical :..

doctor :..

the nurse :..

the hospital :...

medication :...

the syringe :..

the blouse :...

the stethoscope :...

the operating room :...

the pharmacy :...

doctor's office :...

the medical prescription :...

the patient :..

the scanner : ....

ultrasound : ....

the ambulance : ....

the post office : ....

the post office : ....

the mailbox : ....

the postage stamp : ....

the postcard : ....

the envelope : ....

the letter : ....

the computer : ....

the postman: ....

the tompon : ....

the crate : ....

the post office : ....

the parcel : ....

the fax : ....

the phone : ....

school

the schoolbag : ....

the backpack : ....

the pencil case : ....

pencil sharpener : ....

the pencil : ....

the mechanical pencil : ....

gum : ....

the eraser : ....

the ink cartridge : ....

ball-point pen : ....

the graduated ruler : ....

the tube of glue : ....

the pair of scissors : ....

the square : ....

the adhesive tape : ....

notebook : ....

the book : ....

the notebook : ....

the sponge : ....

the chalk stick : ....

water paint :...

the palette :...

gouache tubes :...

the coulor pencils :...

markers :..

the brush :...

leaf :...

the microscope :..

the globe :..

earthly :...

table :..

the rapporteur :..

The compass :...

Table :..

the sticks :..

calculator :..

Game

the marbles :...

spinning top :..

the hoop :...

hopscotch :...

hide and seek :.. ....

the domino :..

billiards or snooker :..

pinball :..

failures :..

lego :..

blind man :..

the leapfrog :..

the yo yo :..

video games :..

the kite :..

the swing :..

the keels :..

frisbee :..

the pedal boat :..

bumper cars :..

the circus :..

skipping card :..

clothes : ....

T-shirt : ....

the dress : ....

the pyjama : ....

trousers : ....

the skirt : ....

Jacket : ....

the coat : ....

the tailor : ....

ballerinas : ....

Sneakers : ....

the sandal : ....

the shoes : ....

the boot : ....

the sneakers : ....

the scarf : ....

the cap : ....

the beret : ....

gloves : ....

Handbag : ....

the backpacks : ....

the tie : ....

the socks : ....

the sock: ....

tights : ....

knitting : ....

underpants : ....

the underpants:

....

the bra: ....

the sweater: ....

the short: ....

the parka:: ....

shirt: ....

the down jacket:

....

the windbreaker

....

the butterfly knot

....

the overalls

....

the uniform

....

the boots :..............................

the belt :..............................

cap :..............................

the shawl :..............................

sportswear :..............................

the veil :..............................

blue jeans :..............................

vest :..............................

trades :..............................

the sacred :..............................

the repairman :..............................

the fisherman :..............................

the potter :..............................

cartoonist :..............................

the flourist :..............................

the Baker :..............................

the carpet seller :..............................

the servant :..............................

the worker :..............................

the banker :..............................

the lawyer :.............................. 77

the director :.............................

the farmer :.............................

The peasant :.............................

the gardener :.............................

filmmaker :.............................

the cameraman :.........................

journal it :.............................

seller :.............................

merchant :.............................

the rescuer :.............................

the tailor :.............................

the photograph :.......................

the painter :.............................

the potter :.............................

the firefighter :.......................

the postman :.........................

Carpenter :.............................

the welder :.............................

the shiner :.............................

the engineer :.........................

doctor :.............................

the dentist :.........................

The veterinarian

....

pharmacy :.........................

the nurse :.........................

the fishmonger

....

the butcher :.........................

the hairdresser

....

the teacher :.........................

the mistress :.......................

The tourist guide :....................................

the air hostess :....................................

the pilot :....................................

the pastry chef :....................................

the bus driver :....................................

the singer :....................................

postman :....................................

the coffee boy :....................................

the truck driver :....................................

the clown :....................................

the policeman :....................................

the musician :....................................

the coach :....................................

the masseuse :....................................

the dresser :....................................

the cooker :....................................

TEST N°2

Try to focus and remember the previous lessons before answering any question

This test includes a set of sentences on different topics. Try to read these random sentences and try to write a dialogue between two or three people

i'm glad to heart that:
me alegro de corazón que
i went on vacation with my family:
me fui de vacaciones con mi familia
we went on trip to spanish:
nos fuimos de viaje a español
that sounds delicious:
eso suena delicioso
it's down town right on main street:
está en el centro de la ciudad justo en la calle principal
nest to the movie theater:
nido al cine
do you ever go comping:
¿alguna vez vas comping?
it's such a good escape from everyday lige:
es un buen escape de la vida cotidiana
cooking over on open fice:
cocinando a la intemperie
but you have to watch out for bears:
pero hay que tener cuidado con los osos
if you make sure you don't leave food out:
si te aseguras de no dejar comida fuera

sounds amazing:
suena asombroso
what kind of play do you like:
que tipo de juego te gusta
shakespeare:
shakespeare
it's such en amazing play:
es un juego increíble
so tragic:
tan trágico
i really hope that i get to go to the word cup:
Realmente espero poder ir a la copa de palabras.
i'm saving up my vacation time at work:
estoy ahorrando mi tiempo de vacaciones en el trabajo
i'm going to have a party to night:
voy a tener una fiesta esta noche
that sounds like fun:
Eso suena divertido

leg:
pierna
sking accident:
accidente de esquí
let's bring her some magazines:
vamos a traerle algunas revistas
sailing:
navegación
i'm a little worried about the weather:
estoy un poco preocupado por el clima
i saw in the weather report that it will be sunny:
vi en el parte meteorológico que hará sol
i want to get stuck in the rain:
quiero quedarme atrapado en la lluvia
me neither:
yo tampoco
instead:
en lugar de
i bet:
te apuesto

when did you get engaged:
Cuándo te comprometiste
ring:
anillo
when are you getting married:
cuando te vas a casar
hopefully:
Ojalá
wedding:
Boda
south pacific:
Pacífico Sur
incredible:
increíble
lawer's office:
despacho de abogados
i'm going to make in to day:
voy a hacer en el día
i should get a raise:
Debería obtener un aumento

we can work something out:
podemos resolver algo
i've had a job offers:
he tenido ofertas de trabajo
how's that spreadsheet coming:
¿Cómo va esa hoja de cálculo?
a bit slow:
un poco lento

a bit slow	:	un poco lento
once	:	una vez
it self	:	sí mismo
to have lunch	:	almorzar
half hour	:	media hora
aroud	:	en voz alta
tough	:	difícil
as long as	:	siempre y cuando
tired of our old boss	:	cansado de nuestro antiguo jefe
he could be so mean	:	él podría ser tan malo
yelling at bob once	:	gritándole a bob una vez
supplies	:	suministros
plenty	:	mucho
boxes	:	cajas
staples	:	grapas
get extra red	:	obtener más rojo
black ones	:	las negras
sticky noes	:	notas adhesivas
glue	:	pegamento

they's going to be holding special election:
van a celebrar elecciones especiales
mayor quit: surfing:
alcalde renunció   surf
might run for president: spring:
podría postularse para presidente   primavera
moved to town:
mudado a la ciudad
i'm totally freaking out:
estoy totalmente enloqueciendo
goffe mug:
taza goffe
it's got a funny cat on it:
tiene un gato divertido en él
i migh have used that earlier:
Podría haberlo usado antes
that explains it:
Eso lo explica
i didn't realize:
no me di cuenta
proposal:
propuesta

bloom: florecer
fall: caer
all th leaves changing color:
todas las hojas cambian de color
windy:
Ventoso
sailboat:
velero
on the lake up north:
en el lago al norte
and doe's it have to be really windy to sail:
y tiene que hacer mucho viento para navegar
mostly cloudy:
mayormente nublado
the day after tomorrow:
pasado mañana
i sure hope:
seguro que espero
well the plants in my garden could really us it(rain):
bueno, las plantas en mi jardín realmente podrían usarla (lluvia)

it has been a while since it rained last:
ha pasado un tiempo desde la última vez que llovió
it's been almos a month and half:
ha pasado casi un mes y medio
i have been watering thim with the hose:
lo he estado regando con la manguera
but it's time consuming:
pero lleva mucho tiempo
what do you have planted : que has plantado
vegetales :vegetales
lettuce :lechuga
onions :cebollas
sledding :trineo
air conditionner :aire acondicionado
it's supposed :se supone
luckily :Afortunadamente
pool :piscina
neighbrhood :barrio
meke it easer to deal with the heat:
Haz que sea más fácil lidiar con el calor
my lawn was all icy this morning:
mi césped estaba todo helado esta mañana

CONCLUSION

The Spanish language you may need at any time, you may want to go on vacation to the country of Spain or complete your studies there, so this book is a comprehensive guide on the Spanish language for speaking with people or writing.

Relax and take your full time learning Spanish or any other language, and you will notice your continuous development, day after day, in mastering the language.

Printed in Great Britain
by Amazon